MW01042305

$WING for the FENCES

An Economic Tale

by PATRICK BURKE

$WING for the FENCES

An Economic Tale

by PATRICK BURKE

BEACON PUBLISHING

SWING FOR THE FENCES

First Edition 2013

ISBN 978-1-937509-59-0

Printed in the United States of America

This book was hand illustrated in
watercolor and ink by Hazel Mitchell

Beacon Publishing
West Palm Beach, Florida 33404
United States of America

TABLE OF CONTENTS

Although I was never much
of a baseball player I hit a home run
when I married my wife Mary Jo.

Thanks for your unwavering
support Mary Jo.

This book is dedicated to you.

1: The Problem

Tommy loved riding his bike home from school, particularly on Fridays. This Friday was especially good not only because it was a warm sunny day for March but also because it was the start of a three-day weekend and the day baseball practice would begin. As he coasted down the long hill into town, watching the changing diamond patterns his front spokes made as they reflected the sun, he daydreamed about hitting the winning home run in the Little League All-Star game. The annual game pitted his Hillsdale Bruins against their archrival, the Riverside Colts, and it was the biggest event in town on Independence Day.

While waiting at a stop sign for his turn to go, Tommy noticed a new display of baseball bats in the window of Haney's Sporting Goods store. He parked his bike at the curb and went in to see if the display included the Z-Comp

Inferno, the new hot bat everyone was talking about. He just knew that bat was all he would need to be the starting shortstop for the Hillsdale All-Stars. His fielding was always top-notch, but his hitting lacked pop. His bat, the aged Moonshot he had inherited from his older brother, Grant, was the culprit, he just knew it.

Tommy grabbed the Inferno from the display and took a couple of full-speed cuts. Mr. Haney was, as usual, all smiles as he walked from behind the counter and said, "That's a beauty isn't it, Tommy?"

"Oh hi, Mr. Haney. It sure is." As Tommy said this he scanned the bat for the price tag. Not finding one, he said, "Mr. Haney, I don't see the price—how much is the Inferno?"

"Yeah, I just put those out and I didn't get a chance to put the tags on them. Let's see, it's right here . . . two twenty."

"Wow, I know my dad won't go for that," Tommy said as he carefully placed the Inferno back on the display.

"I'll tell you what, Tommy, since you and your family are such great customers, I'll let you have it for two hundred, but don't tell anyone, okay?

"Sure, my lips are sealed. Thanks, Mr. Haney, I'll talk to my dad tonight."

Tommy had to leave his bike seat to get up the long hill to his house. As he pedaled, he replayed the discussion with Mr. Haney in his head and decided the discount might be enough incentive for his dad to okay the purchase . . . or maybe not.

That afternoon at practice everyone was enjoying the unseasonably warm day and the optimism and hope that come with the start of a new season. "Hey Walt, think you'll make the All-Star team this year?" Tommy said to his best friend, the team's best player and hitter.

"Hope so," Walt said modestly.

"You're a shoo-in, Walt."

"Not according to my dad. He said every player starts the year with a blank slate."

"Dads and coaches always say stuff like that, but I hope it's true. I spent a lot of time hitting balls off a tee in my basement this winter and I really think I've improved my swing."

Walt, encouraging as always, replied, "I bet that'll pay off big time. I haven't touched a ball or bat since last year; too much football and basketball."

"I hope the practice pays off, and I think it will, but I think I'm going to need a little something extra . . . the Inferno,"

Tommy said as he took a couple of batless swings. "I went to Haney's today and it's in and—it's so cool. It's mostly black with orange and yellow flames, a drop nine sounds about right. I took a couple of cuts with the thirty-one-inch, twenty-two-ounce model and it felt awesome."

"Are you going to get one?"

"I don't know—it's two hundred dollars."

Tommy and Walt's conversation was stopped when the coach called for infield practice. Later, on the short bike ride home, Walt said, "During infield practice I was thinking . . . what if you and I split the cost of the Inferno?"

"You don't have to do that, Walt. You'd hit four hundred with a broomstick."

"Let's buy it together. I already have twenty bucks saved up, so I only need another eighty. Maybe my dad will help out."

Tommy rode in silence for a minute, extended his hand to Walt as they pedaled, and said, "Okay, it's a deal, if I get the okay from my dad. But I've got a feeling he won't spring for a hundred bucks.""Don't you have any money saved up?" Walt asked.

"No, I blew it all on my basketball shoes."

"The way you played this year, I wouldn't call that a waste." Tommy *had* had a good basketball season, but it was over, and as his dad always said, "Yesterday's gone; it's what you do tomorrow that's important."

Tommy replied, "I guess. I'll talk to my dad at dinner tonight and see what he says. I'm not too hopeful. He's a CPA, you know, so he's real tight with money and he loves using it to teach us kids what he calls 'life lessons.'"

"Yeah, my dad is pretty tight too. He says it's all part of his job as a banker."

"You know," said Tommy, "it's too bad our dads aren't professional athletes or rock stars who blow tons of money on all sorts of cool stuff."

When they got to Tommy's street, Tommy and Walt stood over their bikes and shook again on their deal. Before Walt rode away, Tommy said, "I'll let you know how the negotiations with my dad go tomorrow morning at practice."

"Okay. I hope our dads are in good moods."

"Wouldn't hurt," Tommy said over his shoulder as he rode up his driveway.

That night at dinner it was just Tommy and his mom and dad. Grant, a junior at Hillsdale High, was still at lacrosse practice, and his little sister, Amy, a third-grader at Tommy's school, was at a friend's house for a birthday sleepover. Since it was Friday, both of his parents were both relaxed and in a good mood. That, along with the absence of his siblings, who were both louder and more talkative than Tommy, made it much easier for Tommy to bring up the Inferno.

"So, Dad, I stopped in Haney's today."

"I bet Mr. Haney is happy to see spring. All the golfers, lacrosse, baseball, and softball players will be coming in for the latest equipment."

Tommy, happy for an opening, said, "Yeah, he had just put up the display with the new bats before I walked in."

"Did he have anything new? It seems like with sporting goods it's much more about the got-to-have new-and-improved stuff than just replacing worn-out stuff, like it was when I was a kid."

Just as quickly as Tommy had seen his opening, he now saw it closing, until his mom said, "George, you'd think you rode to the sporting goods store on horseback. It seems to me you spare no expense for the latest driver or putter."

"I guess you're right, Ellie."

Tommy breathed a sigh of relief and said, "I took a couple cuts with the Inferno, the latest and hottest bat."

"How'd it feel?" his mom asked.

"Like the answer. My swing has improved a lot from hitting off the tee all winter, but I think this bat will really help my hitting."

His dad, smiling broadly, said, "You sound pretty confident, Tommy. Do you think you can afford it?"

Sensing another perfect opening, Tommy knew now was the time to make his pitch for the bat. "I'd like to. I'm working on a couple of angles."

"I'd think you probably have to. It seems to me you blew . . . er, spent . . . most of your savings on your basketball shoes."

"I had a great season too."

"I think that had more to do with Grant schooling you in the driveway than your shoes.""I'd go fifty-fifty on that, Dad," Tommy said with a smile.

"Speaking of fifty-fifty, is that one of your angles, as in me as your fifty percent partner, Tommy?"

"Actually, no. Walt and I decided we're going to split the cost fifty-fifty and share the bat."

"The way he swings, he might literally split the Inferno," his dad said with a chuckle.

Feeling the tide shifting away from him, Tommy said curtly, "Dad, you can't split a composite bat."

"Okay, Tommy, just kidding. I might be willing to help out. How much is the bat?"

"Mr. Haney said since we're such good customers, he'd give us a discount, but I wasn't allowed to tell anybody."

"Bill Haney, he's quite the salesman. So what's the price?"

"The usual price is two twenty, but he'd sell it to me for two hundred. And since I'm splitting the cost with Walt, I only need a hundred."

As soon as Tommy finished, he knew he hadn't made a strong enough case for his dad to part with a hundred dollars.

"One hundred dollars, huh? I'll tell you what—I'll put up twenty-five if you can put up seventy-five."

"How about you put up forty?"

"How about I put up thirty-five?"

"Okay Dad, you've got a deal," Tommy said as he extended his hand. "Any idea how you're going to make sixty-five dollars?"

"Not really, but I'll think of something. I have to!"

Sensing there might be something in these negotiations for her, Tommy's mom said, "I'll tell you what, since you're off school on Monday, I'll pay you and Grant five dollars each to help me clean out the garage."

"That's five dollars—only sixty to go. This should be easy."

Lying in bed that night, Tommy explained his situation to Grant, who was reading a car magazine at his desk. Tommy and Grant shared a room over the garage. Amy called it the zoo. It did sometimes smell a bit gamey, but he blamed that on Grant's sports equipment.

"So, you need sixty bones, huh? That'll take you months, and no, you can't help with my lawn-cutting business. You're too young. Anyway, I need all the money I can save."

"What do you need the money for?"

"I want to get new wheels for my car and they'll cost at least three hundred."

"I can't see how wheels can be worth three hundred when a life-changing item, like the Inferno, is two hundred, but I guess to each his own, huh, Grant?"

"Right, Squirt."

Grant was right—helping around the house, plus doing odd jobs for the neighbors, would never allow Tommy to earn more than a few dollars per week. At that pace, he'd never have enough money for his half of the Inferno by opening day; he may not even have enough by the All-Star game.

That night Tommy had a vivid dream. There were two outs in the bottom of the seventh and last inning in the annual All-Star game, and the Bruins were down 5–4 to the Riverside Colts. He would either make the last out or be the hero. He was up two balls and one strike when the pitcher threw a fastball that looked to Tommy just like it was sitting on a tee. He hit a towering blast that cleared the left-field fence by ten feet. Just as he rounded third base he felt a tug on his big toe. It was his mom.

"Tommy, get up—it's time for baseball practice." The home run had been a dream, but being awakened for baseball practice was a dream compared with being hauled out of bed for school.

2: The Solution

On the way home from church on Sunday morning, Tommy talked his dad into pitching him batting practice.

"So do you think all that practice over the winter is going to pay off?" his dad asked.

"Hope so, Dad. I know I can hit *your* pitching, anyway," Tommy said as they crossed the street to the middle school ball diamond. Tommy turned his head to see if his dad saw the humor in his remark, and noticed that George had dropped the five-gallon bucket of old baseballs and was after him. Tommy took off and circled the bases before his dad caught him, picked him up, and dropped him playfully at home plate.

"You're out, Tommy, same as you're going to be when I strike you out with my patented George Wilson curve ball."

Tommy's dad had been a high school pitcher—a good one; he had the trophies to prove it. In all honesty, he used his pitching talent to groove ball after ball right into Tommy's wheelhouse, allowing him to hit mostly crisp line drives.

After Tommy dusted himself off, he said, "Dad, I want you to dial up the speed a couple of notches. You know, some of the fifth-graders are pretty strong and can really bring it."

"It never gets easier, does it? You think you'll see many curveballs this year?"

"Paul Evans, our best pitcher, has a pretty good one, but he has a hard time throwing it for a strike."

"Common problem. Still, I'll work in a couple today so you get used to seeing them and don't bail out."

"Okay Dad," Tommy said as he settled into the batter's box.

Tommy's dad, as usual, threw ball after ball right over the plate. Tommy responded with well-hit ball after well-hit ball, except when his dad tossed his curve. This pitch he announced by saying, "Here comes the dark one, Tommy. I hope you can hear it because I know you're not going to see it."

As they were gathering up the balls for the third time, Tommy said, "Let's see, three times, fifty balls, I hit one hundred fifty balls and none left the yard. I need more pop."

As they walked across the street toward home, George said, "Tommy, you've really improved your stroke and your power. You just need to concentrate on hitting the really fat pitches with a little more of an uppercut. That will result in a higher arc and more home runs. Don't worry, they'll come—just don't forget the name of the game is getting on base and scoring, not hitting home runs."

"I know, but I need more power to make the All-Star team. My coach told me I was the best fielding shortstop on the four Hillsdale fourth-grade teams last year, but only the third-best hitter. If I can move up just one hitting spot, I'll clinch the All-Star shortstop position."

"Very doable—just keep up the hard work. Speaking of hard work, it looks like the infrastructure of the new middle school is just about finished. I'll bet the bricklayers will be arriving this week. Now there's a group that knows hard work. You know, I carried hod one summer during high school. It was the hardest thing I ever did."

"I know, Dad, you used to come home and fall asleep on Grandma's front porch before dinner. I'd say you told me that story . . . maybe two hundred times."

Just like that, Tommy's dad picked him up and tossed him into the newly mulched bed in their front yard. "Take that, you ingrate," he said as he sprinted toward their house. "Put those balls in the garage and formulate your cleaning plan for tomorrow," he yelled from the porch.

As Tommy carried the heavy bucket of balls up the driveway to the garage, he thought that except for how tight he was with money, his dad was top-notch.

On Monday, after he finished cleaning out the garage, which, thanks to his mother making a game out of everything, was almost fun, he and Walt met at the middle school with their gloves and a ball.

"Our first burnout game of the year," Walt said as he tossed an easy one to Tommy. As they warmed up, the balls got faster and faster. On about the twentieth throw, Tommy caught one with his palm instead of in the web of his glove and couldn't help letting out a loud "Ouch!"

"That's one for me," Walt said proudly.

"I don't know if this is fair—you throw way harder than me."

"No I don't. I just catch the ball in the web where it doesn't hurt."

Just as his dad had predicted, the bricklayers had arrived that morning, and one of them was walking toward them with a ball that Tommy had just thrown over Walt's head. He stopped about fifty feet away and threw Walt a hard strike that elicited a loud "Ouch!" from Walt.

"One to one," said Tommy.

Walt gave him the *Wait till the adult leaves and we'll see about that* stare.

"So, you boys have been playing a little burnout, I see. Pretty hot today for March. I'm sending one of my men for pop. You boys want one?"

"Sure," they said simultaneously.

"Cream soda for me," said Walt.

"Ditto," said Tommy.

"Cream soda it is. You boys live nearby?"

"I live right across the street," Tommy said, pointing to his house.

"I'm a few blocks over, but Tommy and I practice here all the time. Is that going to be a problem? By the way, my name is Walt, and this is Tommy," Walt said as he shook the man's hand.

"My name is Jeff Adams, and Tommy, I guess my crew and I are going to be your neighbors for a few months. We won't be using the ball diamond for parking or storage, so you boys will have access anytime."

Later, after Jeff handed the boys their cream sodas, Tommy said, "Thanks, Mr. Adams, and nice arm. It takes a lot to get Walt to yell 'ouch.'"

"I've played a little ball in my time. Of course, laying bricks and carrying hod hasn't hurt either."

After their burnout session, Walt and Tommy were sitting on Tommy's front porch finishing their pops when Tommy said, "I've got it."

"What's that?"

"I know how I'm going to make the sixty dollars I need for my half of the Inferno. Since we've got all those thirsty guys right across the street, I'll open a lemonade stand every day after school and before practice. That way Mr. Adams won't have to send someone out for cold drinks every afternoon. I bet I can make sixty bucks in no time at all. I'll run it by my parents tonight."

"Great idea! It's a good thing you're smart and you'll end up with a good job, because I don't know any major leaguers who yell 'ouch' when they catch a ball."

"You don't think a fat pro contract is in my future?" Tommy asked.

"I don't think so," Walt said with a chuckle as he walked toward his bike. "See you at school tomorrow. Truth is, I let out a few ouches with my back turned after a few of your better throws, so you really only lost our burnout game six-four."

Leave it to Walt to say something encouraging. Tommy's dad was right, Walt was just a good soul . . . and a great friend.

3: The Start–Up

That night at dinner, Tommy shared his lemonade stand idea with his family. The responses were predictable.

"Sounds great, honey. I'll make the lemonade," said his mom.

"That would be fun. Can I help?" asked Amy.

"Stupid idea. It'll never work," said Grant.

"That's an interesting idea, Tommy. Do you think it's worth the risk?" asked his dad.

Tommy responded, "What risk?"

"Well, you'll need to do some market research, which means giving away, say, fifty cups of lemonade or so to see if the workers like your mom's recipe. Even then you may not have absolute proof the business will work. You could incur the expense of building the stand only to find out the workers prefer pop."

"Prefer pop to Mom's lemonade? No way!" said Amy, quite confident in her pronouncement.

"Part of starting any new business is taking a risk, Tommy. I'd tend to agree with Amy about Mom's lemonade, but I'd still make a batch tomorrow and test your theory. However, you really won't know if your idea will work until you put it into action. You need to swing for the fences," his dad said with his usual air of authority over all things business.

The next day, Tommy rode his bike home from school as fast as he could. As promised, while he was at school, his mother had made four gallons of lemonade and poured them into half-gallon plastic bottles. She had also stocked

one of the coolers with ice, bought fifty sixteen-ounce cups with lids and one hundred straws, and put all of it in his old red wagon. She had added hand-painted wooden signs to both sides that read TOMMY'S OLD-FASHIONED LEMONADE, and below that she hung a temporary board that read FREE TODAY.

"What do you think?" his mom asked as she walked Tommy outside to show him her handiwork.

"Wow, Mom, that's cool! Thanks a million," Tommy said as he gave her a big hug. He pulled the wagon down the driveway and across the street to the middle school.

As he was setting up shop, as his dad would say, Mr. Adams walked over and said, "So, Tommy, it looks like you're trying to make a buck off my workers."

"That's the plan, but only if today's market research project works out."

"So, free today—then how much tomorrow?"

"I don't know yet." With that the bricklayers were lining up for their free cup of lemonade.

Tommy was encouraged by the responses he was receiving from the workers, who went through all four gallons in less than a half hour, using all fifty cups. Some men even had seconds and thirds.

Tommy raced home with his nearly empty wagon, burst through the back door, and yelled to no one in particular,

"Tommy's Old-Fashioned Lemonade was a home run!"

His mom, who was whipping up a batch of her excellent chili, gave him another big hug and said, "So they like it," as she eyed the empty jugs in the wagon.

"No, Mom, they loved it! I can't wait to open the stand tomorrow. I figure I'll get all the workers plus some walkers if I put the stand at the bottom of our driveway."

"Sounds like a plan. You can hang the wooden signs I made on the old card table from the garage and you're good to go."

"That will be perfect. Wait till I tell Dad how great today's research went," Tommy said proudly.

"Go get ready for baseball practice. I'll drive you today, or you'll be late."

As his dad was finishing his first of what would undoubtedly be two or three bowls of chili, Tommy decided to share his success story. "So Dad, I did my market research after school today."

"Yeah, I saw the wagon with the signs in the garage—quite professional looking. I think I see your mom's artistic side coming out." He turned to Ellie. "Great job with the sign, honey." Then he asked Tommy, "Did the workers like Mom's recipe?"

"They loved it. Some guys even had two or three cups," Tommy said proudly.

His dad looked at Tommy over a heaping spoonful of chili and said, "That's a great indication. Do you have any thoughts on what you're going to charge for a cup?"

"Well, I know the convenience store where the workers buy their pop charges eighty-five cents for a twelve-ounce can, so I figure I need to be somewhere close to that. I guess seventy-five cents seems fair."

"Makes sense," his dad said with a nod.

Tommy continued, "I did some calculations when I got home from practice. I figure I'll have made sixty dollars in under a week."

"How do you figure?" his dad asked with his eyebrows arched.

"Well, I figure thirty cups per day at seventy-five cents each is twenty-two fifty per day, so in just three days, I'd make sixty-seven fifty," Tommy said as he slid his calculations across the table to his dad. George pulled his reading glasses from his pocket, took out a pen and wrote a note on the sheet, and passed it back to Tommy. It read, "What about costs?"

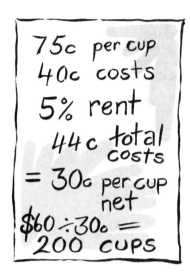

75c per cup
40c costs
5% rent
44c total
   costs
= 30c per cup
      net
$60 ÷ 30c =
200 cups

"Oh yeah, I guess I forgot about that, didn't I?" Tommy grabbed his dad's pen and wrote "costs" on the sheet. "I'll make a list. Let's see . . . lemons, sugar, and water—I guess that's about it. Mom, what does that stuff cost?"

"Hold on, Tommy," his dad said as he pulled the paper back to his side of the table and wrote "lemons, sugar, and water" in a column on the left side of the paper.

"Before we get to the costs of those items, let's figure out what all your expenses will be."

"Like what?"

"What about cups, lids, and straws?" his dad said as he wrote down "supplies." "What else, Tommy? Remember, nothing is free to a business, and the price charged the customer needs to be fair, cover all the costs, and provide a profit that is a fair return on the business owner's time and risk."

"I think I'm getting one of your life lessons," Tommy

said with a look of resignation.

"Just Business 101," his dad said and then added, "So, what are the other costs?"

"Let's see, there's ice, I guess."

As Tommy's dad wrote "ice" down, he asked, "By the way, how do the supplies get to our house?"

"Mom picks those up at McCarthy's market."

"So, you've got transportation costs, including gas, use of the car, and your mom's time."

"But Mom's already going to McCarthy's, so why the extra cost?"

"Tommy, do you think when Mr. Haney orders a box of your prized Infernos, the trucking company that delivers the bats says to him, "Bill, since our truck is passing through Hillsdale anyway, we'll just drop off that box of bats free of charge"?

"When you put it that way, I guess not," Tommy said, warming up to the idea. "I guess I need to figure in the cost of Mom's time making the lemonade too."

"I'll tell you what, I'll train you in exchange for you weeding the flower beds. That way you won't have to pay for my time," said Ellie.

"Okay, Mom, that's a deal."

"No need to outsource if you have the knowhow and the time to do it yourself, Tommy," his dad said, crossing off "production labor," which he had already written on the paper. "Okay, anything else?"

"I think that about covers it, doesn't it?"

"I thought you said you were going to set up the stand with the old card table at the end of our driveway. So, who owns the card table and the driveway?"

"I guess that would be you and Mom, so I guess I need to rent those from you. I'd say a dollar a week should cover it."

"Well, I guess we could figure out what our property taxes, mortgage interest, insurance, and maintenance are for our house and lot, and then figure out what percentage the driveway apron is to the total value, or . . ."

"Or what?" Tommy asked, not liking the sound of all the calculations involved in figuring out a fair rental for the table and apron.

"Let's say I just charge you five percent of your sales. That way, if you don't do as well as you're planning, you won't have a fixed cost to worry about."

"Fixed cost?" Tommy said quizzically.

"Costs that don't vary with the amount of sales are called fixed costs. On the other hand, variable costs go up and down with the sales volume."

"But if I do really well, then I could be paying you more rent than I should."

"That's true, but you'll have less risk if we base the rent

on your sales level."

"Less risk, I like the sound of that," Tommy said, writing "5%" next to the rent expense line.

While Tommy and his dad were compiling the expense list, his mom was costing out the lemonade recipe. "Okay boys, I have your figure. Based on the price of lemons, sugar, bottled water, cups, lids, straws, transportation costs, my recipe costs about forty cents for twelve ounces of lemonade, which fills a sixteen-ounce cup that already has ice in it. I'll throw in the ice since we never use all the ice our icemaker churns out anyway."

"Thanks for calculating the costs, Mom—that's a big help. And thanks for the free ice. Any objection to that, Dad?"

"Let's just call that my contribution to your enterprise. Now, let's see, if we use your seventy-five cents figure, subtract forty cents for your product costs and five percent for rent, your total costs are about forty-four cents, so you'll net about thirty cents per cup. So, how many cups will you have to sell to earn sixty dollars in profits?"

Tommy spoke as he did the math, "Sixty dollars is six thousand cents, divided by thirty cents profit per cup, equals two hundred cups. Wow, that's more than twice as many as I thought, but I still think it's worth my time."

"How so?" his dad asked, showing a little pride in Tommy's grasp of Business 101.

"I figure if I sell just twenty-five cups per day, which I think is low, and multiply that by thirty cents, I'd be making seven fifty for the hour or so I'll be selling the lemonade after school. That's more than Grant makes mowing lawns!"

Grant, who had been uncharacteristically quiet until now, chimed in, "Nice try, chump—how about your time to make the lemonade the night before? That's got to be at least an hour."

"Oh yeah, so I guess that takes my hourly profit to three seventy-five. That's still not bad, even if it's not what you earn, Grant," Tommy said defiantly.

"At three seventy-five per hour, it will take you about twenty hours to earn enough money for the bat. Is that Inferno worth that to you?" his dad asked, shrugging his shoulders.

"Absolutely! It's not just the bat, Dad, it's making the Hillsdale All-Star team, and that's priceless!"

4: Competing

"Let's see, that's eighteen dollars in singles, plus sixty-three quarters—that's another fifteen seventy-five. So, Dad, my total sales for my first day were thirty-three seventy-five. That's exactly what I thought, since I counted forty-five cups sold."

"Great day, Tommy. So at the thirty cents per cup in profit, you netted thirteen fifty after all your expenses."

"Are you sure, Dad?" Tommy said, always amazed at how fast his dad could do math in his head.

"Yep, I'm sure. Maybe you're right, you could have enough money for your Inferno in a week or so—but don't count on it."

"Things went pretty good today, but a few problems did come up."

"Like what?" his dad asked, obviously pleased with Tommy's effort and interested in adding his ample business knowledge.

"Well, for one thing, I didn't have any quarters to make change for the first few customers, so I had to track them down later. I also ran out of ice, so I think I can improve my product and service and cut down on my time. I had to ask Mom to drive me to baseball practice again because I didn't have enough time to ride my bike."

"Pretty minor problems," said George. "Although one day does not a successful business make, I'd say you've got a pretty good chance at making a go of it."

"Thanks, Dad," Tommy said as he transferred his first day's earnings from the cigar box to an old coffee can, obviously proud of his take. "Is it okay if I pay you back for

the ingredients, supplies, and rent at the end of the week?"

"Sure, Tommy. I'll give you terms on your account."

"Terms?"

"That's business talk for a supplier, namely me, giving you time to pay your bill. Otherwise, I'd expect payment at the time of delivery."

"Okay, Dad. Thanks for the terms."

On Thursday, Tommy rode his bike home as fast as he could, not only because he wanted to make sure he had enough time to sell lemonade and get to baseball practice on time but also because the dark clouds looked like rain was not far off.

The cloudburst started just as the workers were lining up at the stand. Some stayed and bought a cup of lemonade, but most ran for cover. Tommy, seeing no more customers were likely, closed up shop. After stowing his stand in the garage and bringing all the lemonade and supplies into the kitchen, he looked forlornly into the cigar box at the day's measly receipts. He could count it without even taking it out of the box. "Four fifty . . . terrible, and no baseball practice today—also terrible."

His mom dried his hair with one towel and wrapped another around his shoulders. "There's always tomorrow. Leave your shoes on the mat and go change your clothes. I'll put the lemonade in the fridge."

"Will it still be good tomorrow?"

"It should last three days or so. We'll need to keep that in mind as we map out your production schedule. If we have to throw away any product, that will reduce your profit," said

Ellie, proud of her command of business lingo thanks to being married to George all these years.

"I guess that's right. I have to pay for all the lemonade—I guess Dad would call it inventory—even if I don't use it."

"You can't worry about it, Tommy. It's all part of doing business," his mom said, putting her arm around his shoulder.

"It's like Dad said, business is about risk management."

It was still raining the next morning, and it rained all day. Tommy stared gloomily out his mom's car window as they were riding home from school. "Thanks for picking us up, Mom," Amy said from the backseat, trying to break the somber mood. "It's no fun walking home from school in the rain, especially with a full backpack. Can we stop at the coffee shop for hot chocolate?"

"No, but I'll make some when we get home. Mine's better anyway."

With that, Tommy snapped out of his gloomy mood and said, "That's it—I'll sell hot chocolate today."

"Oh no you won't. It's a good idea but I don't have enough supplies. Anyway, the workers wouldn't want to wait in line in the rain."

"I could deliver it," Tommy said enthusiastically.

"Sorry, Tommy, the forecast for Monday is warm and sunny. You can reopen then."

"Okay, but I still think it's a good idea."

That night at dinner Tommy shared his idea of adding hot chocolate to his product offerings with his dad.

"I don't think it would be worth it, Tommy. You'd need to wait for another cold, rainy day to do your market test. And then there's the problem of keeping the product hot and needing to go back and forth between hot chocolate and lemonade, which would likely result in your inventory spoiling. I know you and Mom discussed this, but having inventory go bad would result in reduced profits."

"I guess you're right. I just hate to miss a day. It just adds one more day until Walt and I can get the Inferno."

In order to lighten the mood, Tommy's mom said, "Speaking of Walt, how's he doing with his half of the money?"

"He said he'd have enough in about a week, so it'll be my fault that our purchase of the Inferno is delayed," Tommy said with resignation.

Just as his mom had promised, Monday was warm and sunny. Expecting a great sales day, Tommy was especially excited as he streaked home from school on his bike. Also, as his mom predicted, sales were great; he brought in over forty dollars.

Tommy finished counting his receipts and put them in the coffee can. Looking at the almost full can, he could practically feel the Inferno in his hands as he daydreamed about hitting the game-winning home run.

"So, Tommy, considering two days of rain, it still looks like you're doing pretty well for your first week."

"I'm about halfway there, and I checked the long-term forecast and the rest of the week is supposed to be rain-free and pretty warm. By the way, Dad, here's your forty dollars to cover this week's costs. Looks like I made over twenty five dollars!"

"Great! I bet tomorrow will be another great day like today. Go ahead and grab your glove and get going to practice."

As Tommy rode his bike to practice he thought about the ups and downs of the first week of business and decided his lemonade stand wasn't just a way to make money; it was also interesting and fun. Then and there he decided his new business would be the topic of his personal experience essay assigned for Tuesday.

Just after the bell rang to begin school on Tuesday morning, Mrs. Kelly asked if anyone wanted to read their essay to the class. Tommy raised his hand and said, "I would, Mrs. Kelly."

He walked confidently to the front of the classroom and read his essay about what he referred to as his thriving retail business.

That night at dinner he bragged to his family about another good day in sales. "Thirty-four fifty—not bad, huh Dad?"

"Great, Tommy. By the way, did you read your essay about Tommy's Old-Fashioned Lemonade to the class like you promised?"

"I did and I think I did a really good job explaining my business. I went through the recipe, and how much I paid for the ingredients and supplies. I even explained how you were charging me rent based on my sales. The class seemed really interested." What Tommy didn't know was there was one person in the class, Polly Stevens, who was perhaps a bit too interested. Polly needed money to buy herself a new lacrosse stick, and since she was too young to babysit, she was only able to make money by helping her mom with household chores.

"I hope you didn't give away any trade secrets," George said as he cleared the plates.

"I never thought of that. . . . That's weird, I just felt a shiver." At that very moment, Polly and her mother were putting the finishing touches on the POLLY'S OLDE-TYME LEMONADE sign for her own lemonade stand.

Just as forecasted, Wednesday was sunny and warm, and Tommy was whistling as he stocked his stand. He was ready for a big day of sales. When he flipped his sign to OPEN, a few workers streamed toward the stand. Expecting a rush, he began filling cups with ice, ready to pour quickly. It turned out he only needed a few. As the ice began to melt, he checked his watch and saw that it was time to pack up his stand so he wouldn't be late for baseball practice. It was on his last trip to the sidewalk that he noticed something: Several of his usual customers were tossing pink cups into the Dumpster. He quickly crossed the street to investigate. Mr. Adams walked over to him and said, "Tough break getting competition so early, Tommy." With that, the bricklayer tossed his pink cup on top of the dozen others in the Dumpster.

"What do you mean?"

"Some girl named Polly opened a stand on the street bordering the other side of the parking lot. If you look through the trees you can see it," Mr. Adams said, pointing over his left shoulder. She calls it "Polly's Olde-Tyme Lemonade," which he pronounced "Old-E Time-E."

"Polly Stevens; I should've known. She got the idea from the report I gave in school yesterday about my lemonade stand. How come she got so much business?" Tommy asked, eyeing the growing load of pink cups in the Dumpster.

"Well, she cut your price by a dime and her lemonade,

I hate to say, is just about as good as yours, maybe a little sweeter."

"I guess my dad was right," Tommy said with a sigh.

"How's that?"

"I suppose my essay gave away what my dad called trade secrets."

Mr. Adams said, "My dad always said competition brings out the best in everyone. I'm sure you'll think of something, Tommy."

Tommy was waiting at the back door as his dad parked his car in the garage. No sooner had he put down his briefcase than Tommy started in, "Dad! Dad! You were right, I gave away my trade secrets."

"So, how was school, your stand, and baseball practice?" George said slowly, trying to calm Tommy down.

"Good, bad, and good, and I need to talk to you about the bad."

"Okay, I assume you mean your stand. What happened?"

"Polly Stevens stole my trade secrets, opened a stand, and is charging a dime less for sweeter lemonade and stole a bunch of my customers."

"Just the law of supply and demand, Tommy," his dad said, shaking his head.

"I've never heard of that law."

"Sure you have—we discussed it when Mr. Haney had

to fight off that competitor in Riverdale by cutting his prices. Don't you remember?"

"Oh yeah. I thought you were saying 'Surprise the Band'—you know, the game they played on those old Johnny Carson DVDs you and Mom got from Grandma. I never could figure out what that had to do with Mr. Haney and his competition," Tommy said, shrugging his shoulders.

With that his dad broke into one of his patented laughing fits. "That's hilarious! You're right, your mom loved those DVDs. Actually, that part of the show was called Stump the Band, but your mom called it Surprise the Band. Anyway, the law of supply and demand states that when the demand for a product, like your lemonade, stays the same and the supply increases with a new source, like Polly's stand, the price will naturally go down."

"So, I'll lower my price to fifty-five cents and drive her out of business," Tommy said with conviction.

"Not a good idea. Your profit would go down to only about ten cents per cup, hardly worth your time. Competing on price alone is a race to the bottom. Bring it up at dinner. I bet someone in this family will have an idea."

During dinner Tommy retold his story and asked for everyone's ideas.

Grant said, "Pack it in, Squirt—no bat for you."

Mom said, "Let's see, how could you make your product different?"

"I've got it," Amy said confidently.

"Okay, let's have it," Tommy said, interested in any idea that would result in getting his hands on the Inferno.

"I've notice that sometimes Mr. Adams sends someone out even though you guys are selling them drinks."

"What does the man who goes out buy?" Tommy said, not quite believing his little sister caught something he didn't.

"Snacks!" Amy said triumphantly. "I bet none of them are as good as Mom's oatmeal chocolate chip cookies. My idea is keep your price at seventy-five cents for the lemonade and charge, say, thirty-five cents for the cookie, but offer them both together for, let's say, a dollar."

"I get it—great idea, Amy! I'll call it Tommy's Double Play."

"Out of the mouths of babes," his dad said, giving Amy a big hug.

"I'll figure out my cost and bake a batch tonight for tomorrow, Tommy," his mom said excitedly.

"I guess Mr. Adams was right," Tommy said to his dad as he was loading the dishwasher.

"How so?"

"He said competition brings out the best in everyone."

"Smart man—that's why he's the foreman. Improving your product or adding other needed products is a natural outcome of competition. Customers are better served and the most innovative company wins."

"I'll do my market research test tomorrow and start selling them on Friday. That'll teach Polly! I'll bet I drive her right out of business!"

5: Diversification

While Tommy was at school on Thursday, his mom baked a hundred cookies. After school, Tommy set up his stand as usual and Amy put the cookies on several large plates, which she then placed on an auxiliary table at the stand, just above a sign that read TOMMY'S MOM'S OLD FASHIONED OATMEAL COOKIES . . . SERVED BY AMY, and below that, TAKE ONE. FREE TODAY ONLY. Almost every customer asked for at least one cookie. Amy wrapped each cookie in a napkin and asked every taker to let her know if they liked it. To no one's surprise, the cookies received rave reviews from all the customers.

Tommy's stand, despite the competition from Polly, sold thirty cups of lemonade. He had to admit he was pleased that his cookie promotion had put a significant dent in Polly's business.

Tommy gave the last customer his change and turned to

Amy and said, "I need to get going. I've got a game tonight so I have to get to the field early for warm-ups. You'll have to put the stand away by yourself. You've seen what I do, so it shouldn't be a problem." With that, Tommy sprinted toward the house, and seconds later was zipping by Amy on his bike as she was dragging the cooler up the driveway. "Thanks, Amy! The cookies were a great idea," Tommy said as he turned onto the street.

Amy responded, "You're welcome," to the back of Tommy's helmeted head, which was by now a half block up the street.

Tommy had a great game against the Ludlow Mudcats, who they beat 5–2. He started two double plays and hit a single and a double. Walt drove him in both times. Walt followed his run-scoring double in the second inning with a ball that hit the top of the fence and rolled halfway to third before the left fielder finally tracked it down. Walt never stopped running, and was rounding third as the left fielder made his throw home. The ball reached home just before Walt began his picture-perfect slide. The Mudcats catcher's tag barely missed Walt's toe—an inside-the-park home run.

Tommy and Walt were sitting on their bikes rehashing the game. "You know, your inside-the-parker would've been ten feet over the fence if you had used the Inferno," said Tommy.

"Maybe. Same result anyway. I'll have my half of the money by tomorrow. If you do too, we can go to Haney's on Saturday and get the bat."

"I had a pretty good day today. I'll tally up my earnings so far and try to figure out what I'll make on Friday, and let you know tomorrow."

That night during dinner, the conversation was, as usual, free flowing, especially from Amy.

"Just like I thought, all the men thought Mom's cookies were the best they'd ever tasted."

"Amy, I think they were just trying to be nice," said Ellie.

"No, Mom, I could tell they meant it," Amy said, adding, "So, Tommy, what have you decided to charge for the cookies?"

"Mom, did you figure out the cost yet?" Tommy asked.

"Including my valuable time, they cost twenty cents each to make," his mom responded with a wink.

"I guess I'll charge thirty-five cents each and a dollar for the Double Play—a lemonade and a cookie. Do you think that's enough of a deal to make sure I outsell Polly, Dad?"

"I'd say so; you'll make fifteen cents per cookie if that's all they buy, and thirty-five cents if they buy a lemonade and a cookie. Not bad at all, Tommy."

When Tommy and Amy opened the stand on Friday, they stuck a sign in the front yard, next to the stand, that read TOMMY'S DOUBLE PLAY—LEMONADE AND A COOKIE FOR ONLY $1. Just like Wednesday, business was great. They sold thirty-three lemonades and twenty-five cookies. Tommy counted the cash and said, "Amy, today's take was thirty-one dollars. Here, take two dollars for your work yesterday and today. Since you did such a great job putting away the stand yesterday, I want you to do it again today." With that Tommy jumped on his bike, which he had parked next to the stand, with his glove already hanging from the handlebars, and sped off.

That evening after practice when Tommy burst through the back door, his dad and Amy were sitting at the kitchen table. His dad was wearing his dark blue terrycloth bathrobe over his shirt and tie, and was holding the meat tenderizing mallet. "The Wilson family court is now in session," he said as he tapped the table with the mallet. "The court will now hear the case of Amy Wilson versus Tommy Wilson. The plaintiff Amy Wilson's complaint contains two claims. Number one, that the defendant, Tommy Wilson, engaged in an unfair labor practice by making the plaintiff put away the lemonade stand by herself for two straight days; and claim two, that the defendant has failed to pay the plaintiff a fair wage for her time working at the stand."

Tommy immediately realized by the look on his dad's

face that, despite the bathrobe and meat mallet, he was quite serious.

"Does the defendant wish to offer any defense to these claims?" his dad asked, still with a serious look in his eyes.

Tommy stared at his shoes and said, "No, guilty as charged. Sorry Amy, I guess I took advantage of you."

"The court suggests Tommy pay his sister Amy four dollars per day, and an extra two if she is required to put away the stand alone. This should ensure your help in the future, right Tommy?"

"Heck yeah! Two dollars is way too much to pay to have Amy put the stand away."

By this time, Grant and his mother were standing in the doorway leading to the family room, listening to the proceedings and trying to stifle a laugh.

George continued, "Good, case closed. Let's eat dinner. And by the way, Tommy, good employers not only pay their employees fairly; they also treat them fairly. You know, showing respect to your sister costs you nothing and means a lot to her. Right, Amy?"

"Right, Dad," Amy said as she put her arm around a humbled Tommy's shoulder. Tommy sighed and began setting the table.

The weather on Monday was sunny and warm and Tommy had high hopes for a big day of sales. While he was setting up his stand, he noticed the parking lot was crowded with unfamiliar pickup trucks. His first customer was Mr. Adams.

"Hi Mr. Adams, do you have some new bricklayers working today? I see a lot of unfamiliar trucks."

"No, those are the finish carpenters. They're going to work on the wing we just finished while we start the next one. I've told the foreman all about you and your stand. Get ready for a really big day—it's warm inside and I'm sure the carpenters are really thirsty." Just as Mr. Adams had predicted and Tommy had hoped, Monday was a record-setter. Tommy and Amy sold sixty cups of lemonade and forty cookies, racking up fifty-five dollars in sales. Tommy was able to keep his stand open until almost five o'clock since practice was canceled. Grant pulled into the driveway during the last, and biggest, rush of customers of the day. Instead of going into the house for his customary post-lacrosse and pre-dinner sandwich and two large glasses of milk, he decided to help Tommy and Amy with the stand.

"Hey, Tommy and Amy, who's the new guy, the boss?" asked Tim Jones, one of their best customers.

"Nah, that's just my goofy big brother, Grant," Tommy said with a chuckle.

Grant had to admit he was amazed with not only Tommy and Amy's easy rapport with the customers but also the significantly overstuffed cigar box.

That night at dinner, Grant complimented Tommy and Amy on the obviously great day and added, "I guess you made enough for your bat, huh, Tommy?"

"I guess, Dad and I will go over my finances after dinner, right Dad?"

"Right. A fifty-five-dollar day should put you close to your goal."

"I'll tell you what, Tommy, how about I take over the stand now that you've made enough money for your bat so I can supplement my lawn earnings and get my wheels faster?" Grant said hopefully.

"No way! But I do have an idea for you to make some money off the workers," Tommy said with a sly smile.

"Oh yeah? What's that?" Grant asked, obviously interested, but not liking Tommy's smirk.

Before I tell you, I think we should discuss what my part of your profit should be," Tommy said, arching his eyebrows at a flummoxed Grant, who could respond only with a death stare.

George, seeing a storm brewing, said, "Grant, before you get upset, hear Tommy out. You have to understand, through his hard work, and later Amy's, they've built an excellent reputation for satisfying their customers. In short, 'Tommy's' is now a valuable brand."

"I guess you're right, Dad. Okay, Tommy, let's hear your idea."

"Well, I've noticed all the pickups in the lot are filthy by Friday, but they're all spotless on Monday. I figure most of the workers spend a lot of time over the weekend washing their trucks—time they'd rather spend fishing or playing golf. I bet if you opened 'Grant's Hand Wash at Tommy's,'" he said, making air quotes, "on Thursdays and Fridays, you could make a fortune."

Grant stared at Tommy slack-jawed and said, "Tommy, that's not a bad idea. Dad, would you mind if I used the driveway to wash cars?"

"Okay with me; however, I have two requirements. One, you need to do a really good job to preserve the value of Tommy's brand, and two, the workers have to drop off and pick up their trucks. I don't want to risk you wrecking one."

"That's a deal! I know from your deal with Tommy and Amy, I'll need to pay you for water, supplies, and rent for the driveway. Let's say I charge seven dollars per truck and pay you two dollars for expenses and a dollar to Tommy for . . . what would you call it, Dad?"

"I'd call it a royalty and a fair deal."

"I'll take it! How about you, Tommy?"

"If it's good with you, Dad, I'll accept it," Tommy said as he extended his hand to Grant, who shook it and squeezed hard enough that Tommy wanted to wince, but he didn't, which he knew irked his big brother.

"Tommy," George said, "I'll tally up your profits and see if you've made the sixty-five dollars you need for your half of the Inferno. If you have, I'll take you and Walt to Haney's tonight to pick it up."

Later after Tommy, Grant, and Amy finished the dishes,

their dad walked into the kitchen and said, "Tommy, call Walt—you two are going to be the proud owners of the Inferno. Tell him we'll pick him up in five minutes."

"All right!" Tommy exclaimed. "I bet I hit one out of the park tomorrow night!"

Tommy and Walt ran from Haney's entrance straight to the bat display. Tommy grabbed the Inferno and handed it to Walt. "Go ahead and take the first cut."

Walt obliged and said, "Feels like pure power." Walt put the bat to his ear and said, "Inferno here says you're getting your first four-bagger tomorrow night."

As Tommy and Walt took turns swinging the bat, George was counting out the two hundred dollars, which was, unfortunately, mostly in dollar bills. After he and Mr.

Haney concluded the transaction, George said, "Let's go to the middle school ball diamond and I'll pitch you two some batting practice."

"Thanks, Dad. Let's go," Tommy said to Walt, sprinting through Haney's parking lot and swinging the bat over his head like a war club.

Tommy was up two balls and one strike at his first official at bat with the Inferno. Being behind in the count, the pitcher was a little too careful and grooved a pitch "right down Broadway," as Tommy's dad called a pitch over the center of the plate. It looked like a beach ball to Tommy, who hit it with the thickest part of the bat, making a satisfying *thonk* sound, indicating a well-hit ball. The ball traveled like a frozen rope until it hit the center field fence. Tommy coasted into second with a stand-up double. Walt was up next. The pitcher, now rattled, served up what Walt later called a cupcake. Walt promptly deposited said cupcake twenty feet beyond the left field fence and directly into an unsuspecting fan's thirty-two-ounce cherry slushy. Even the Bayside Bombers fans got a laugh out of what looked like a scene out of *Ghostbusters*. Tommy's team won 6–2, and he hit another double, but still . . . no home run.

The stand did a brisk business on Wednesday. That evening, Grant made a sign indicating his cleaning service would be available Thursday and Friday, which Tommy stuck in the lawn next to the stand. Several customers seemed interested. The weather cooperated and Grant was able to wash five trucks on Thursday and seven on Friday.

Friday night at dinner, George announced to the family that because of the success of Tommy's stand and its related businesses, he was seriously considering early retirement. All agreed that Dad might be a little optimistic. However, Grant, in a rare show of generosity, offered to buy the family milk shakes at Riley's. As the others piled into the car, George put his arm around Tommy and said, "Tommy, you have really shown me something by the way you've turned a simple lemonade stand into a thriving business. I'd say your future as a businessman looks bright, indeed."

"Maybe so, Dad, but what I really want to do is hit a home run."

"I know, Tommy. That'll come, but for now you should be happy your business is a grand slam."

6: The All-Star

Near the end of a rare Saturday practice, Tommy's coach, Mr. Simms, gave Tommy's jersey a tug and said, "Walk with me for a minute." With that they strolled behind the backstop and sat in the first row of bleachers. "Tommy, you're really having a great season. Your fielding is, as usual, excellent and you've really improved your hitting."

"Thanks, Mr. Simms. I worked hard on it all winter. It seems to have paid off. I still don't have a homer this year, though. I was sure my new bat would be the difference, but I've only hit a bunch of doubles and one triple."

"Well, the other coaches have taken note of your improvement and voted you the starting shortstop for Wednesday's All-Star game."

Tommy was speechless. Finally, he was able to get out a misty-eyed "thanks" as he shook Mr. Simms's outstretched hand.

"You, Walt, and Paul are going to represent Hillsdale in Wednesday's Independence Day game. I'm also happy to report that I've been selected to coach this year's team."

As they stood up, Mr. Simms said, "I've already told Paul and Walt they made the team. Do your best—we've lost the last two to Riverside and it's time we turn it around."

Tommy walked back to the field and noticed Walt and Paul were waiting for him next to the first base foul line. When Tommy got about five yards away, Walt and Paul ran at him with fists pumping. The three engaged in an elaborate exchange of high, low, and medium fives, as well as various fist bumps. Paul finally said, "Welcome to the Hillsdale Bruins All-Stars, Tommy. It's time we showed Riverside who plays the best baseball in this part of the state."

Walt, who looked even happier than Tommy, chimed in, "With a slick fielding shortstop like you, and with Paul's blazing fastball, we're definitely fielding a team that can get it done."

"Having the best hitter around shouldn't hurt," Paul said, clapping Walt on the back.

On the bike ride home from practice, Tommy decided he would add some drama to his All-Star announcement by waiting until his dad got around to asking him how his day went during dinner.

That night, just as Tommy stuffed an extra-large bite of fried chicken in his mouth, George said, "So Tommy, how was your day?"

"I made the *alshtar* team!" Tommy responded.

"You did what?" his dad asked.

Triumphantly, Tommy, having swallowed his chicken, replied, "I made the All-Star team, Dad!"

The whole table applauded, even Grant.

"Oh, Tommy, that's wonderful," said Ellie.

"I'm so happy for you," said Amy.

"I'm very proud of your effort, Tommy. It's nice to see it was recognized," said George.

"Finally stepping out of my long shadow," said Grant, who punctuated it with a shot to Tommy's shoulder.

As usual, the Little League All-Star game between the Hillsdale Bruins and the Riverside Colts was a titanic struggle. The stands at Hillsdale High, which hosted the game every other year, were packed with boosters for both teams. It seemed every player's aunts, uncles, grandparents, siblings, and, of course, parents were there to root loudly for their team.

It was the bottom of the seventh and final inning and the Hillsdale Bruins trailed the Riverside Colts three to two. Walt, who was, of course, batting cleanup, was the first batter. He scorched a two-one pitch into the left field power alley

and slid into third for a lead-off triple. This Hillsdale fans, sensing a comeback, began cheering loudly at every pitch. Unfortunately the next two batters struck out on six straight fastballs from Riverside's amped-up starter, Rod Williams. Tommy strode to the plate, trying to look confident. He took the first pitch for a called strike and fouled the second pitch straight back—a good sign that he had figured out Rod's speed. With the count now 0–2, the Riverside players were smiling and nodding at each other confidently. Just before Rod started his windup, Tommy asked the umpire for time. Tommy stepped out of the batter's box and looked over to third base at Walt, who gave him a clenched fist, showing his support. As he stepped back into the box, Tommy heard his dad yell, "You own him, Tommy!" Tommy was confident Rod would throw another heater, and he was just as confident he'd put the fat part of the Inferno on the ball just in front of the plate.

Tommy could see from the rotation of the seams that Rod had indeed thrown him another fastball, right down Broadway. Tommy strode toward the ball and laid a lick on it like no other ball he'd ever hit. He watched hopefully as the ball arched toward the Haney's Sporting Goods sign painted on the left field fence. The Riverside left fielder, who was playing in, not respecting Tommy's power, had no chance to catch the ball. The only question was in or out of the park. The ball finally came down, bounced on top of the fence, and fell . . . into the stands. The Hillsdale faithful howled with delight as Tommy ran the bases for his first homer, a walk-off in the annual All-Star game. His teammates barely let him tag home before mobbing him. Just like that, Walt and Paul had him on their shoulders. Tommy had to brush tears from his eyes as he saw his family cheering loudly from the stands. It was the best moment of his life.

Tommy's stand and all related businesses continued to operate successfully through the summer. Although he spent some money here and there on a movie or a video game, he really wasn't keeping track of his earnings. He, Amy, and Grant became good partners and even better friends.

Although the stand had started out as a means of making money, Tommy now realized that pleasing people was also a worthy goal, and even more motivating than the profits.

On a Friday in late August, just a week before school was to start, Tommy's dad came home from work early and helped the kids take down the stand. As they were stowing the last pieces away, George asked Tommy to help him unload something from the back of his SUV. Since Grant and Amy were already inside, whatever was in the truck was going to be up to just his dad and him to handle. George hit the unlock button and Tommy opened the back door of the SUV, and there was the most beautiful eighteen-speed mountain bike he'd ever seen.

"Dad, are you taking up biking?"

"No, Tommy, it's for you. I took some of your profits and added a few bucks of my own and negotiated a bit with Mr. Haney. It's last year's model, so he gave me a friendly price. You like it?"

Tommy had pulled the bike out and was now astride the "Red Cyclone." "It's awesome, Dad! Thanks a million. Honestly, I didn't think I'd need a new bike since I'll be walking right across the street to the new middle school."

"That's part of the rest of the surprise. I'll be making an announcement at dinner tonight." George put his arm around Tommy's shoulder and said, "The bike is just my way of saying how proud I am of you and the success you made with your business this summer."

Once the family had tucked into Ellie Wilson's famous spaghetti dinner, George tapped his water glass with his fork. "I've got a little announcement to make. First, congratulations to all of you kids, not only for successfully running a business, but also learning to work together. I'm unbelievably proud of you. Now I'd like to report that you kids weren't the only ones saving for something special around here. Your mom's parents decided to move to an apartment closer to town and your mom and I agreed to buy their house."

The kids all looked at each other and let out an "All right!" in unison.

Although their grandparents' house was a mile or so out of town, it had a large yard, and most important, a pool with a diving board and a slide.

"So, when's the move, Dad?" asked Tommy.

"Next week. So, Tommy, I guess you'll need to tell your customers they'll have to go to Polly's after next week. So now you know why you'll need that new bike—your ride to school will be close to two miles."

"That's okay, it'll be fun on the Red Cyclone."

Later, after all the dishes were put away, Tommy approached his dad and said, "Thanks again for the new bike. It's the coolest. Also, I've got a business question for you."

"Shoot."

"I've heard you tell stories about helping clients sell their businesses, right?"

"That's right, I do it several times each year. Why?"

"Well, they're starting to build the new fire station a block from Polly's house and Polly never did add cookies to her menu. I know most of the workers preferred Mom's lemonade to hers, so she might like to buy our recipes. What would accountants call stuff like that?"

"They'd call it intellectual property and a great chance to make a little more money . . . maybe seed money for next summer's business. You should work out a fair split of the price with Amy since the cookies were her idea and I know she has plans for a business of her own. "

"Okay, that's fair. How about seventy-five percent me and twenty-five percent Amy?"

"No, let's say sixty you and forty Amy. After all, you got a new bike."

"You're right—sixty-forty it is. I'm going to need some seed money because I've got some really big ideas for next summer's business."

As Tommy ran upstairs, his dad wiped a tear from his eye. Tommy thought his All-Star homer was the highlight of the summer, but his dad knew better. Based on how successfully he ran his stand during the summer, Tommy was well on his way to becoming a business All-Star too!

t

ABOUT THE AUTHOR

Patrick Burke is a lawyer, CPA and serial entrepreneur. As the Managing Partner of Burke & Schindler PLL, a CPA and business consulting firm in Cincinnati, Ohio, Patrick has been helping entrepreneurs start, run and exit businesses for thirty years. He is a frequent lecturer and media commentator on business and entrepreneurial issues.

If you liked *Swing For The Fences* you may also like Patrick's adult business parable, *Exit Velocity: An Entrepreneur's Quest for Financial Freedom*.